Our Faith Journey - Battling with Intellectual and Physical Disabilities

---

J U N E   L I M

Co-Authors:

Gabriel and June Lee
(Parents of Bryan and Charmeine Lee)

Richard and Helen Boey
(Parents of Jonathan Boey)

Steven and Shwu Huey Sum
(Parents of Garren and Gavin Sum)

An Enabling All to Fish project

To order additional copies of this book, contact
Toll Free +65 3165 7531 (Singapore)
Toll Free +60 3 3099 4412 (Malaysia)
www.partridgepublishing.com/singapore
orders.singapore@partridgepublishing.com

Because of the dynamic nature of the Internet, any web addresses or links contained in this book may have changed since publication and may no longer be valid. The views expressed in this work are solely those of the author and do not necessarily reflect the views of the publisher, and the publisher hereby disclaims any responsibility for them.

Scripture quotations marked NIV are taken from the Holy Bible, New International Version®. NIV®. Copyright © 1973, 1978, 1984 by International Bible Society. Used by permission of Zondervan. All rights reserved. [Biblica]

ISBN
ISBN: 978-1-5437-7288-3 (sc)
ISBN: 978-1-5437-7290-6 (hc)
ISBN: 978-1-5437-7289-0 (e)

Print information available on the last page.

04/03/2023

PARTRIDGE

After reading the book, I am amazed at how God has intervened and miraculously saved his life and at Jonathan's courage in fighting and overcoming the odds stacked against him. Jonathan has been such a blessing and his laughter often brings unspeakable joy to others. It is my earnest prayer that Jonathan's story will inspire, encourage, and impact others to make a difference in their own lives. God is the ultimate healer, and his life has shown what is impossible for man to do, God can do it (Luke 1:37). All Glory to the Lord!

Tan Chin Lee
An itinerant Evangelist of Living Sanctuary Brethren Church

We have seen how God has been so faithful to them, helping them and strengthening them each step of the way. We are very happy to see Garren growing bigger and stronger. While the years ahead may still be challenging, we are assured that the faith that Steven, Shwu Huey, Gavin and Garren have in God will certainly bring them forward to a bright future. They are excellent testimonies for our Lord Jesus Christ.

Paul & Pushpa Ou Yong,
Former Cell Leaders of Steven and Shwu Huey

Life isn't always easy. We face many different challenges all the time. But one thing that makes life that bit easier is knowing that you don't have to go through it alone. I am tremendously proud of how Gabriel, June, Bryan and Charmeine have come together to share not only their story, but the story of many others who have walked this journey. I pray that these stories will teach us how to come alongside families with special needs, as well as show us that we never need to walk alone.

Rev Daniel Khong
Senior Pastor, Faith Community Baptist Church

As we read through Bryan's milestones and breakthroughs, these are clear evidence of God's faithfulness in his life. God has a purpose for Bryan and his family. We thank God for giving us this opportunity to know them and may we continue to witness more breakthroughs together as one spiritual family.

Eric Chow and Arlene Aw
Cell Group Leaders of Gabriel & June

May this book inspire us to better understand the world of those with special needs and their families so that we recognise the uniqueness, value and worth of every single one of them and play our part to love and support them. Indeed every child is created in the image of God and children are a blessing from God.

Rev Poh Wee Long and Pastor Cristabel Poh
Pastors, Faith Community Baptist Church

CONTENTS

INTRODUCTION

Ring . . . The ringing of the alarm clock is heard. With this sound, it's the mark of the start of yet another busy day.

As we go about our daily lives, one will wonder what and who goes by and what impact each experience brings and forms our life experience. At times, life passes by too quickly that we do not take time to slow down to 'smell the flowers' and appreciate the things and people we have. It is also through such slowing-down and seeing things from other's perspective that allow us to surface out the God-given compassionate side in each of us.

It is never easy for parents to hear doctors labelling our children as having special needs, diagnosing them as having Global Development Delay, Down Syndrome, Cerebral Palsy, or Intellectual Disabilities. Do many adults or typical children know what these children are going through?

We believe every human being in this world has a purpose and should be given that chance to live out that purpose. The birth of this book is God-led, and we pray that each biography of these children, written in a simple but sincere way, will inspire and encourage each reader in a personal manner one way or another.

We wish all readers to have faith in all difficult situations they may face. Readers will also understand and accept these children with special needs for who they are. Society will focus on their strengths, learn from the positive characters traits of these children and not their disabilities.

Every faith journey has its amazing story to share, especially these children. We pray God will use these amazing children to do His wills through the sharing of their stories, preparing them to be God's ambassadors.

THE BIRTH OF THIS BOOK

What inspired us to get started?

As a mother of a child with special needs, things around us tick very differently. In addition, as an educator for children with special needs, a lot more has been impressed upon my thoughts and emotions.

Through every lesson I taught my son and students, I can see their positiveness to learn, persevering spirit and joyfulness, as well as their individual limitations. Yes, indeed, despite their many learning disabilities, these children are human too, and they have the will and grit to face life's challenges; if only their families and society are there to render support to allow these children to bring out their 'never give up' spirit in them.

I have been asking myself and Gabriel, how do we share such amazing characters with the rest of the parents and children? How do we, as parents or educators, help these children to be accepted in this fast-moving technology society? All these thoughts kept howling at us until God showed us the people we should look for and the direction to go.

Thank God for Garren's and Jonathan's parents, Steven and Shwu Huey and Richard and Helen who agreed to join us on this journey. In July 2022, we started penning down our children's biographies and looking for a publisher. As parents who are all first-time writers, we came together to share our thoughts and pen down this amazing life journey. Along this faith journey, despite our busyness and many trials encountered, we managed to press on and completed this book.

Gabriel and June Lee
Parents of Bryan and Charmeine Lee
Founders of Splendore Montessori Pte Ltd
(Early Intervention and Enrichment Learning Centre)

THE BIRTH OF THIS BOOK

What inspired us to join in?

One Saturday afternoon, when we dropped off Jonathan to attend the class of Ms. June, an experienced teacher teaching children with special needs, she popped a question to us, whether we are interested to join in a project to publish a book for young children to create awareness of children with special needs.

We thought and prayed about it and agreed to participate. Even though we know our government and society is gaining momentum in accepting people with special needs, we felt there are still some areas that may require a little more work, especially awareness in young children who may not have opportunities to interact with children with special needs.

We started to write our stories, and as we go on, we realised all the children in this book have one thing in common—that is they all experience God's healing and blessings. With this, we understood this project is not only to create awareness but also, more importantly, to glorify and be thankful to our Almighty God, Lord Jesus Christ.

Richard and Helen Boey
Parents of Jonathan Boey

THE BIRTH OF THIS BOOK

What inspired us to join in?

We wanted to share with others Garren's life story and his fighting spirit against many challenges. This allows us to share with other parents who may be in similar circumstances, that all is not lost and hope is there if we continue to have faith in the God we trust.

Steven and Shwu Huey Sum
Parents of Garren and Gavin Sum

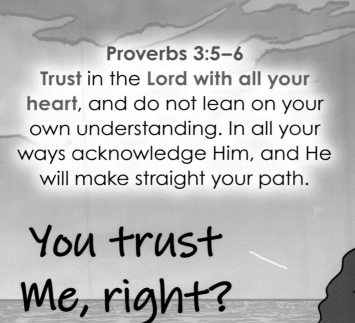

Proverbs 3:5–6
Trust in the **Lord with all your heart**, and do not lean on your own understanding. In all your ways acknowledge Him, and He will make straight your path.

You trust Me, right?

Yes!

Dear God, thank You for being the light of the world and going with us through the trials. Help us continue to trust in You, shine our light and do amazing things that will bring You glory.

BRYAN LEE

Cerebral Palsy and Intellectual Disability

Hi, everyone! I am Bryan.
I am twelve years old.

When I was three months old, I had severe seizures, known as Infantile Spasms. The medication for treating my seizures had impacted my learning. My brain was affected. I was **empty-bottled**, and I needed to learn everything from scratch.

How Blessed Is My Life

After two years of continuous consumption of the medication, I lost the opportunity to **learn** and see the world like other children. Battling with Cerebral Palsy and Global Development Delays, I needed **100 percent** assistance from my parents and sister to look after me. I was **totally dependent** on them.

Despite my learning delays, I am **blessed** to be able to learn like a typical child. My family members **did not give up** on me, although I am **different** from other children. Despite **all eyes** were on us whenever we head out, they will still bring me to see and explore the world out there. They prayed **persistently** and **helped** me go through every difficult and impossible **obstacle**. I am **blessed** with loving family members, pastors, church leaders, many uncles and aunties who have been praying fervently for me over these years. Thank you, everyone, for **loving** me!

Areas I Overcame **(Miracle Breakthroughs)**

- Develop **eye contact** with others at **4** years old
- **Swallow and drink** like typical children at **5** years old
- **Crawl and sit** on my own and **call** Papa and Mama at **7** years old
- **Know** numbers till 100 and addition at **9** years old
- **Spell** 15-letter words at **10** years old
- **Babble** '**Amen**' and '**Praise God**' at **11** years old

I Can **(My Strengths and Things I Like to Do)**

- I am cheerful.
- I am a people observer and say 'hi' to people around me.
- I have a never-give-up spirit.
- I can match 7 sequential images accordingly.
- I play soccer and games with the help of my mummy and sister.
- I read books together with my daddy.
- I listen to worship songs.

I Cannot (My Weakness)

- I cannot control my hands as they can be stiff, and they don't listen to me.
- I cannot walk on my own as my body muscles are not strong enough.
- I cannot express my words and feelings to others as I am still babbling for most of my speech.

Do Not . . .

- Ignore me when I say 'hi' to you—I'm just being friendly.
- Look at my ankle foot orthoses (AFOs) attached to my feet as I need these as walking support.
- Look at me in a weird way.
- Be angry when my **uncontrolled** hands touch you.

I Am No Different from You (I Want To . . .)

- Use my hands to do things like you do (feed myself, play with toys, write, etc.)
- Walk and run in the garden on my own
- Talk about my days and feelings to the people around me
- Play and interact with people around me
- Learn things like other children
- Worship, dance, and praise God

In Summary

As a boy with Cerebral Palsy and Intellectual Disability, as much as I want to be like all of you, I have my limitations. I hope the people around me and those I meet would understand and accept me for who I am. However, I am hopeful and I believe I can overcome all challenges as I know my God will deliver me.

Words for Learning

different	not the same as other people
persistently	continuously
obstacle	barrier, hurdle
loving	feeling or showing love or great care
uncontrolled	happening or done without being stopped
give up	admit defeat
empty-bottled	nothing is left
totally dependent	requires someone's full support on the daily life activities

You can do it!

Deuteronomy 31:6
Be strong and courageous. Do not be afraid or terrified because of them, for the Lord your God goes with you; he will never leave you nor forsake you.

PRAYER CHANGES THINGS

Dear God, thank You for showing Your unconditional love. Help us be strong and courageous, knowing Your word and being reminded to live like You every day.

CHARMEINE LEE

Hi, everyone! I am Charmeine.

I am Bryan's sister.

How Blessed Is My Life to Have Bryan as My Brother

He is an **adorable** and **handsome** boy. Although he is slow in learning compared to his peers, in my eyes, he is a smart and entertaining boy. He likes to listen to worship songs, which we often do together. The way he calls me "姐姐" (sister) makes me love him so much.

Whenever I feel stressed over my studies, Bryan is always the one to bring me laughter. The smile on his face gets me going. Whenever I see him going through so many **obstacles**, yet he does not give up on himself, this **persevering spirit** of his encourages me a lot.

How do I feel when having a sibling different from others?

I am so fortunate to have Bryan as my brother. Though he is not as playful as other boys, he taught me how to be a **responsible**, **resilient**, and **empathetic** girl. Bryan makes me look at things in a different way and react differently. He is a caring boy—he will show comfort to people he sees crying or feeling sad. I wish he can spread his handsome smile and love to others.

I feel people need to learn to be more **selfless**. Bryan started to be "labelled" and "judged" when he was three months old till now. **All eyes are on him** when he goes out of the house. Rather than giving us a "weird" look when we bring him out, do treat us as normal people. Who would like to have a child or sibling with special needs? But everyone **yearns** to be healthy and clever.

I remember there were times when Bryan fell sick and his muscle control and learning developments went **downhill.** We came to realise that there are people out there who are not concerned about flu-cough symptoms. However, these flu-cough symptoms can seriously cause the immune system of a child with special needs to become worse and even cause a loss of life. I feel we should be more selfless and express care to the needs of those with special needs and their parents.

It's sad to see Bryan and other children with medical conditions deteriorate in their development because of such lack in social responsibility.

My Prayers

(I pray that miracle breakthroughs will happen to Bryan.)

- Communicate with other people as he loves to talk
- Use his hands to do the things as he desires to do
- Walk **independently** as he loves to be in the community
- Spread his handsome smile and love to others so others may learn to love one another
- Go up the stage independently to glorify God's wonderful name

Words for Learning

responsible	having an obligation to do something or having control over or care for someone as part of one's job or role
resilient	(of a person or animal) able to withstand or recover quickly from difficult conditions
empathetic	showing an ability to understand and share the feelings of another
selfless	concerned more with the needs and wishes of others than with one's own
downhill	deteriorating
independent	able to do on your own
persevering spirit	continuing to do something despite difficulty or delay in achieving success
all eyes are on him	everyone is looking at someone or something

Mark 11:22–24

So Jesus answered and said to them, 'Have **Faith in God**. For assuredly, I say to you, whoever says to this mountain, "Be removed and be cast into the sea," and does not doubt in his heart, but believes that those things he says will be done, he will have whatever he says. Therefore I say to you, whatever things you ask when you **pray, believe** that you receive them, and you will have them.'

Shield of Faith

Dear God, thank You for answering our prayers. Help us to always believe and put my faith in You.

JONATHAN BOEY

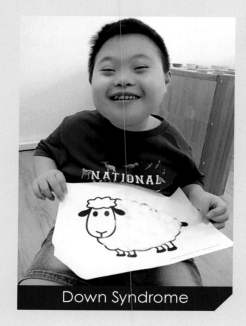
Down Syndrome

Hi, everyone! I am Jonathan. I am nine years old.

I have a genetic abnormality, having an extra chromosome in my DNA. The medical term is Trisomy 21 or Down syndrome. Because of the genetic abnormality, I was born with the following medical issues: leukemic cells in my blood and a hole in my heart.

Leukemia

Because of the traces of leukemic cells found in my blood, I must visit an oncologist, a doctor who specialises in treating cancer, every month after birth to check on my blood count (red blood cells, white blood cells, and platelets). After I celebrated my first birthday, my blood count started **deteriorating,** and the oncologist recommended me to begin chemotherapy treatment. It was a time of **uncertainty** as the oncologist **advised** that I may not respond well to the treatment as they have checked that I lack certain proteins in my blood that are helpful in chemotherapy. However, our God is in control of the situation, and I completed the three-month treatment without much side effects and have been healthy ever since. Only God has the final say. He is in control.

A Hole in My Heart

When I was two months old, a paediatrician, suspected I have a hole in my heart, and I was then referred to a cardiologist, heart doctor, for advice and confirm the diagnosis. My parents were told by the cardiologist that the hole is moderate size, and there are two scenarios according to his experience. The best case would be the hole will close when I reach three years old, or it will get worse and require surgery. After my second appointment with the cardiologist, he **advised** my parents he would see me six months later as there was no change in my condition. I went to see the cardiologist six months later, and one week prior to the appointment date, God **impressed** on my parents to read the Bible (Mark 11:22–24), and it reminded them that we are to ask in our prayers and believe that we will receive it and God will deliver. One week later I went to see the cardiologist, and to his surprise, the hole disappeared. All of us, my parents and the cardiologist, celebrated with tears of joy and thanksgiving to our Almighty God who has healed me. The cardiologist was surprised by this **miraculous healing** as I was just eight months old with underlying medical issues.

How Blessed Is My Life

- I am thankful to God as He knows best all the things in my life.
- I am loved by my parents who take care of me and never give up on me.
- God, in His **perfect** time, provided me a healthy heart when I was 8 months old so I was able to go for chemotherapy.
- God is a **faithful** God, and He has provided my family everything, including provisions for my medical bills. The chemotherapy I went through cost many thousands of dollars, but it did not cost a single cent to my family as the government included chemotherapy treatment in my health insurance in the year I was born.
- God knows everything. He is in control.

Areas I Overcome **(Miracle Breakthroughs)**

- **I walked** when I was **2 years and 3 months old**, even though I have low muscle tone.
- **I had good appetite** and have **gained weight.** I was very skinny and had difficulty in drinking milk when I was **born**.
- **I can express** that I need to go to the toilet to poo when I was **5** years old.

I Can (My Strengths and Things I Like to Do)

- I am a joyful boy.
- I can dance and sing.
- I watch children's programs on the iPad.
- I like eating McDonald's French fries.
- I love being with my family.

I Cannot (My Weakness)

- I cannot read, write and talk properly.
- I cannot stay focused on my work.

Do Not . . .

- Stare at me when I seem to be shouting—I am trying to express myself.
- Rush me. Please allow me to take time to speak as I am still learning.

I Am No Different from You (I Want To . . .)

- Be understood and accepted for who I am by the people around me and those I meet
- Be hopeful and believe God is working in my life
- Overcome the challenges as I know my God will deliver me
- Worship, dance, and praise God

In Summary

As a boy with Down syndrome, I have my limitations, and I hope the people around me and those I meet understand and accept me for who I am. However, I am hopeful and I believe I can overcome all challenges as I know my God will deliver me.

Words for Learning

deteriorating	becoming worse
uncertainty	the state of unknown
advised	offer suggestions about the best course of action to someone
impressed	feeling or showing admiration or respect for someone or something
express	convey a thought or feeling in words or by gestures and conduct
gain	Obtain
miraculous healing	a type of faith healing in which cures appear
perfect	having all the required or desirable elements, qualities, or characteristics as good as it is possible to be
faithful	remaining loyal and steadfast

Luke 11:9–10
So the Lord say to you:
Ask and it will be given to
you; **seek** and you will
find; knock and the door
will be opened to you.
For everyone who asks
receives; the one who
seeks finds; and to the
one who knocks, the
door will be opened.

God made each of us different.
My walk with God
is filled with hope.

Dear God, thank You for showing us a glimpse of heaven through Your amazing miracles of healing. Help us continue to ask and seek You.

GARREN SUM

CCHS, GDD,
Neuromuscular scoliosis

Hi, everyone! I am Garren.
I am fourteen years old.

When I was born, I was diagnosed with Congenital Central Hypoventilation Syndrome (CCHS), which simply means I will forget to breathe or have very **shallow breathing** when I go into deep sleep.

When I was three months old, I have to go through tracheostomy operation, cut a small hole in my throat, to insert a trachy tube that is tied to my neck. This trachy tube is connected to a ventilator machine to help me breathe when I am sleeping.

I was also diagnosed with Global Developmental Delay (GDD). Having **low muscle tone** and flexible ligament **impacted** my mobility and movement on my hands, legs, and body, also affecting my swallowing and chewing ability. I am still unable to speak.

When I was seven years old, I was diagnosed with epileptic seizures and required to start medication since then to try to control my seizures.

Faith comes by listening to His Word!

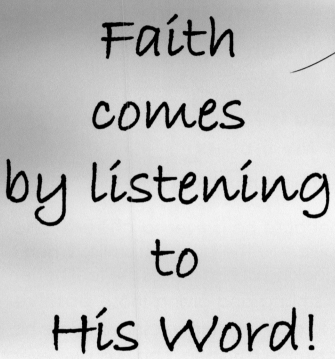

2 Corinthians 5:7
For we **live by faith**, not by sight.

Dear God, thank You for being with us whenever we face difficult situations. Help us continue to put our faith in You and know that You are always there.

GAVIN SUM

Hi, everyone! I am Gavin.
I am Garren's brother.

How Blessed Is My Life to Have Garren as My Brother

I love my brother as much as I hate him.

I love him because he is ever so **cheerful**. He will always give you the brightest smile. When I don't feel that great or feeling low, just looking at him makes me feel better almost instantly because he is always smiling and giving those **positive vibes**. And he is always using his way to play with him by showing me his 'angry' face. I am pretty sure he could be the **bubbliest** boy you will ever meet, and I guess his world is so much pure and beautiful. Perhaps I could say my brother is the light, the star, the sun of this family, shining through our hearts, keeping this family together.

I hate him because he is always making everyone **worried** for him, and in quite a fair bit of occasions, we thought we might lose him. I see my parents so worried, so **anxious** to a point/verge of going crazy. This just breaks my heart, or I should say it's **tearing my heart into many pieces**.

I have been the only child in this family for many years till he came along. I thought I am finally getting a companion, a person to have fun growing up with. But instead, he put me into an expressway of growing up. I got to grow up fast and be mature fast. In his younger days, he got hospitalised quite often that I learnt how to be independent, how to take care of myself, how to cook, how to not create even more worries for my loved ones. Nevertheless, he is my brother. We have the same blood flowing through us. And I have the responsibility to care and protect him as much as I can.

How do I feel when having a sibling different from others?

When I was younger, I hated it when people gave a weird look when they saw my brother to a point that I wanted to shout back at them to say, "What are you looking at? Do you think he wished to be born like this?"

But as I grew older and as time passed, I just started to **ignore** it and not take it to heart. After all, there's really nothing much I can do about it.

If a person is diagnosed with cancer, you wouldn't laugh and joke about it. Then *why* are people with special needs or even those with mental issues **discriminated**?

I feel people need to start to have more **empathy** towards others, especially people with special needs. No one would wish to be born like this, no one deserves to receive such treatment.

And another group of people that should be empathised with or cared for are the caregivers/family members of these children with special needs. They are truly the **heroes** behind the scenes, facing not only the amount of pressure but also in terms of financial.

I have read countless articles about how these family members could not take the pressure and ended their own lives. If this world can just show that bit more of care, concern, empathy and sympathy, perhaps this group of people, family members of children with special needs, won't be crushed by the immense pressure society is giving them.

My Wishes

(I pray that miracle breakthroughs will happen to Garren.)

- Walk, run, and jump
- Talk and call every one of us
- Go up the stage without support to glorify God's wonderful name

Words for Learning

cheerful	noticeably happy and optimistic
bubbliest	(of a person) full of cheerful high spirits
worried	anxious or troubled about actual or potential problems
ignore	fail to consider
discriminated	differentiated
sympathy	feelings of pity and sorrow for someone else's misfortune
positive vibes	feelings of energy that someone delivers
tearing my heart into many pieces	to cause one an unbearable amount of grief, sadness, or distress

Printed in the United States
by Baker & Taylor Publisher Services